21 Ways I Run Away

an ode to the things that give me solace

Meher Gill Sandhu

BookLeaf Publishing

India | USA | UK

Dedication

To the pastimes, people and places that give me peace.

Preface

"21 Ways I Run Away" is a collection of poems honoring all the pastimes, people and places that give me comfort and calm. These poems are an illustration of how they help me unwind. This anthology was written to display my love and admiration for all these activities and to try to spread this passion to help others find their own. As you read through the rhymes, I hope you find as much peace and tranquility as I found while writing them.

Acknowledgements

I want to thank my family for their constant encouragement and motivation. I am also deeply grateful for all the people who acted like editors and offered their crucial feedback and support. And to everyone who reads these poems, thank you, I hope you enjoy.

Books

A book,
its pages,
eternal,
unbending.

A world,
a realm,
to delve,
to forget.

To be,
to see,
to envelop,
to breathe.

To become,
to indulge,
in a world,
to succumb.

Writing

My pen glides
on its white dance floor,
and it leaves its marks
as my mind soars.

The words tell stories
and open my eyes,
as I uncover
what's in my mind.

And on this page
within its walls,
I can finally understand
my heart's calls.

And as I pour
all that I feel,
out on this page
I start to heal.

Daydreaming

In my mind
I make up tales,
I work out
all the details.

I create stories
that help me see,
anything I want
I can be.

I get to choose
the course of events,
the time and place
and how it presents.

And while I daydream
and pretend,
the chaos in my mind
finally ends.

Drawing

I scrape my pencil
across the page,
and as I do
I feel like a mage.

With my wand in hand
I can create,
any image
that they narrate.

I sketch people, places,
and even things,
and as I do
it feels like I've been given wings.

I use my gift
to exhibit,
everything around me
that I call my favourite.

Painting

As the colour
fills the sheet,
my vision and reality
finally meet.

The scene in my mind
slowly takes shape,
the white turns into
a beautiful landscape.

The paint fills the canvas
and showcases my passion,
a scenery created
by my imagination.

Slowly the brushes
bring together my vision,
the image in my mind
for everyone to envision.

Photography

With a click
I can capture,
the views around me
that enrapture.

I can preserve
the memories forever,
so that I can
look back at them whenever.

I can even change
how the moment feels,
by changing the angle
from which it appears.

This small invention
helps me protect,
past adventures and places
that I select.

Puzzles

Every piece,
has a place,
a fixed spot,
a specific space.

Every piece,
it is important,
without even one,
the puzzle is nonexistent.

Every piece,
is carefully placed,
cautious fingers,
even in my haste.

Every piece,
helps create,
the final picture,
something great.

Origami

The paper is smooth
beneath my hand,
every move I will take
has already been planned.

The paper will fold
again and again,
over itself
it will give me zen.

You could make anything
from the square,
and it will appear
seemingly from thin air.

In the end
it will become,
a masterpiece
from a conundrum.

Crafts

There are so many options
and things I could create,
so many materials I could use
and mediums I could collate.

So many designs I could utilize
and methods to employ,
so many techniques I could follow
and ideas I could deploy.

It helps me harness
my creativity,
free my imagination
from its captivity.

The outcome is
a design I've crafted,
and the learnings I've made
that can now be gifted.

LEGO

I put every block down,
every brick,
every piece I choose,
I carefully pick.

They all have,
a certain spot to be,
and I follow the plan,
to the T.

The order calms me,
it gives me peace,
the structure leads,
the chaos to cease.

In the end,
I have invented,
something new and steady,
that I have constructed.

Games

There are so many games
that one could play,
so many types and rules
and different displays.

Some I can
play alone,
quiet and calm
in the zone.

Some I can
play surrounded,
by the people who care
to keep me grounded.

All these games
their steps and techniques,
will create memories
that give joy for weeks.

Swimming

I am enveloped,
the water surrounds,
as I float,
the water grounds.

As I drift,
as I glide,
the water gives,
calm to my mind.

I flow with the water,
I move with the waves,
all the hurdles that will come,
I feel I can brave.

And as I submerge,
in the bright blue,
I feel like,
I have been born anew.

Dancing

I flow with the sound
as the music plays,
my body moves
I'm in a daze.

I glide across
the cold, hard floor,
the music lifts me
and I soar.

I sway and spin
and turn and twirl,
along with the music
I unfurl.

My body moves
with the sound,
and in the music
I am found.

Music

The music flows,
the music lifts,
in my mind,
it slowly drifts.

The music picks me up,
it guides,
my soul and body,
slowly glides.

The music leads me,
it shows me the way,
throughout the cold and dark,
of everyday.

The music helps me,
it defends,
against the dark,
it gives me a friend.

Piano

My fingers press,
these ivory keys,
black and white,
they move with ease.

There are only 12 notes,
but endless permutations,
these 12 notes create,
the most beautiful foundations.

I play a melody,
chords and notes,
different progressions,
the sound floats.

These keys evoke feelings,
they evoke joy and calm,
they create lifelong memories,
underneath your palm.

Singing

The words leave my mouth
and float,
through the air
every note.

My voice turns into
an instrument,
it makes harmonies
however intricate.

Every lyric
every line,
every verse
and every rhyme.

They heal me
they help me hone,
my thoughts and feelings
with every tone.

Baking

All the ingredients
I collect,
I measure
and recheck.

Everything
is perfectly placed,
I mix them all
and give it a taste.

And then I put it in the oven
to give it heat,
and I take it out
when it's ready to eat.

The smell wafts through the air
it fills the room,
and there's a taste of heaven
in every spoon.

Math

It starts with numbers
as they create,
their own language
and open a gate.

To another dimension
that opens your mind,
and answers to questions
you can find.

If you learn,
how to apply,
every problem
you can try.

It gives a sense of serenity
as you complete,
obstacle after obstacle
on the sheet.

Languages

Every new word
that I learn,
helps me
at some turn.

They get added
to a list,
that helps me
coexist.

With every new syllable
and every new sound,
a new way to express
my thoughts is found.

Learning these different languages
gives me a way,
to really perfect
what I want to say.

Travel

Every place
that I go,
helps me and
my mind to grow.

I get to learn
about different people and regions,
their culture, traditions,
and past legions.

It expands my knowledge
as I gather perspectives,
to gain different views
it is very effective.

Each place I visit
teaches me something new,
and shows me the world
is larger than I ever knew.

Conversations

I start to talk
my mind flows,
on and on
the conversation goes.

The topics change
and stories continue,
questions arise
and discussions ensue.

I am surrounded by comfort
and its warm embrace,
while we sit here
face to face.

The voices calm me
and I succumb,
the chaos in my mind
is overcome.